A  TRUE

MAKING AND SAVING
MONEY

JOBS, TAXES, INFLATION...AND MUCH MORE!

Janet Liu and Melinda Liu

Children's Press®
An imprint of Scholastic Inc.

Content Consultant
Dr. Marie A. Bussing
Emeriti Faculty, Romain College of Business
University of Southern Indiana

Library of Congress Cataloging-in-Publication Data
Names: Liu, Janet, author. | Liu, Melinda, author.
Title: Making and saving money: jobs, taxes, inflation . . . and much more! / by Janet and Melinda Liu.
Description: First edition. | New York, NY: Scholastic, Inc., 2024. | Series: A true book: money! | Includes
   bibliographical references and index. | Audience: Ages 8–10. | Audience: Grades 4–6 | Summary: "A
   series to build strong financial habits early on in life! How can I make money? What is inflation? What
   is the difference between a debit card and a credit card? Economics—and more specifically, money—
   play such a large role in our lives. Yet there are many mysteries and misconceptions surrounding the
   basic concepts of finance and smart money management. This A True Book series offers students
   the know-how they'll need to start on the road to financial literacy—a crucial skill for today's world.
   Interesting information is presented in a fun, friendly way—and in the simplest terms possible—which
   will enable students to build strong financial habits early on in life. Knowing about different jobs and
   how to make the most of their earnings are just two critical financial literacy skills that all kids should
   have. Did you know that doctors have some of the highest paying jobs in the United States? Or that
   just 39 percent of kids in America have a savings account? Learn all this and more in Making and
   Saving Money—a book that gives kids insight into how our economy works."—Provided by publisher.
Identifiers: LCCN 2022054145 (print) | LCCN 2022054146 (ebook) | ISBN 9781339004907 (library binding)
   | ISBN 9781339004914 (paperback) | ISBN 9781339004921 (ebk)
Subjects: LCSH: Saving and investment—Juvenile literature. | Money—Juvenile literature. | Finance,
   Personal—Juvenile literature. | Taxation—Juvenile literature. | Inflation (Finance)—Juvenile literature. |
   BISAC: JUVENILE NONFICTION / Concepts / Money | JUVENILE NONFICTION / General
Classification: LCC HG179 .L5395 2023 (print) | LCC HG179 (ebook) | DDC 332.024—dc23/eng/20221220
LC record available at https://lccn.loc.gov/2022054145
LC ebook record available at https://lccn.loc.gov/2022054146

10 9 8 7 6 5 4 3 2 1   24 25 26 27 28

Printed in China 62
First edition, 2024

Design by Kathleen Petelinsek
Series produced by Spooky Cheetah Press

Find the Truth!

Everything you are about to read is true *except* for one of the sentences on this page.

Which one is **TRUE**?

T or F The price of chocolate chip cookies has not changed in the past 40 years.

T or F People with jobs pay income tax.

Find the answers in this book.

What's in This Book?

The **BIG** Truth

Salary is one thing
to consider when
picking a job.

How much money we spend affects how much we can save!

Mikaila Ulmer started a business when she was just a little kid.

INTRODUCTION

Money is important for everyday life.
We use it to meet our **needs**—like buying groceries and clothing or paying for housing. And we use it to buy things we **want**, like vacations and video games. **Many families try hard to save extra money** for the future. Of course, in order to spend or save money, most people first have to make it! That is why people go to work—to earn an **income**.

In the United States, 26 million bills, or **currency** notes, are printed every day!

The largest U.S. bill in circulation today is the $100 bill.

Making money is important. **So is learning about the different things that can affect our earnings.** Some things, like taxes, affect how much of our income we actually have to spend or save. Others, like inflation, affect how much our money is really worth. **Knowing how to make money and knowing how to save it are important life skills.** And they are skills you can definitely learn. Turn the page to get started!

About 61 percent of kids in the United States get an allowance.

The concept of an allowance was made popular in the United States in 1912.

Making Money

Some children get an allowance. That is a fixed amount of money that a parent or caregiver gives to the child every week or month. Some kids also have jobs outside the home. Certain jobs are just right for young people. Other jobs are only for adults. Most people try to choose their jobs based on what they are good at or what they love to do—like helping sick people or making movies. They also take **salary** into consideration.

The Job Market

In the United States, doctors and surgeons have the highest salaries. Top earners make more than $300,000 on average every year. Fast-food workers make the lowest salaries, as do the hosts at restaurants. They earn about $24,000 per year. Teachers fall in the middle, making an average salary of about $65,000 per year.

Many teachers don't have to work over the summer.

In America, child labor laws limit the types of jobs kids under 18 can have—and the number of hours they can work.

A lot of kids do chores to earn their allowances.

Teenagers can't be doctors or teachers. But there are many jobs that kids can have. In the United States, kids can start working at certain jobs when they turn 14. For example, they can babysit or take care of a neighbor's pet. Those jobs can often be found by speaking to neighbors and friends.

"Yes, my prices are high, but how else am I supposed to buy a Boulevard M109R? Certainly not on my allowance."

The word "entrepreneur" comes from the French word entreprendre, which means "to do something."

The child selling lemonade has priced a glass at $500 to quickly earn enough money to buy a motorcycle. Do you think that strategy will work?

Be an Entrepreneur!

A job is a good way to make money. You might also consider becoming an **entrepreneur**— someone who launches and runs their own company. Being an entrepreneur can come with high rewards. If your business is successful, there may not be a limit on how much money you can make. However, owning your own business also comes with high risks. If your company does not do well, you might not make any money at all.

A Sweet Buzz-ness

Anyone can start a business—even a little kid! Mikaila Ulmer was stung by a bee when she was four years old. Then she was stung again less than a week later! Mikaila became afraid of bees, so she decided to learn more about them. That is how she learned about the important role bees play in our ecosystem. When Mikaila entered a children's business competition, she gave the bees a role in that too. Mikaila took her great-granny's lemonade recipe and added in some honey. That was the start of Mikaila's company, Me & the Bees Lemonade. Today, Me & the Bees Lemonade can be found in stores and restaurants around the United States. And Mikaila donates a percentage of every bottle sold to organizations that work to protect honeybees.

Starting a Business

Interested in running your own business? First, talk to your parents or another trusted adult. They may have good suggestions for how to get started. Then determine which **goods** or **services** the people around you might need or want. For example, do you want to make and sell cookies? What about starting a business to mow your neighbors' lawns? Consider what skills—and how much free time—you have, and then pick the business that works best for you.

Washing cars can be a fun way to earn money!

Making a solid business plan will set you on the road to success.

Next, create a business plan. That is a document that explains your product or service and your plan for making money. The business plan should include estimates for the cost of starting your business and the price you will have to charge customers in order to make a **profit**. It should also include ideas for how to advertise your product or service.

Businesses with one owner are called sole proprietorships. They make up 73 percent of all businesses in the United States.

Discrimination in the Workplace

Discrimination is unfair treatment of people because of race, ethnicity, religion, gender, or age. For decades, many women and people of color in the United States faced discrimination in the workplace. Two important laws were passed to address that problem.

THE EQUAL PAY ACT OF 1963

Women have always been paid less than men— even when they are performing the same job. That is a form of discrimination. In 1963, the U.S. Congress passed the Equal Pay Act to combat this problem. The law states that people who perform equal work should receive the same pay, regardless of gender.

THE CIVIL RIGHTS ACT OF 1964

Historically, people of color and women have had less access to jobs than white men have had. They have also been less likely to be promoted. In 1964, President Lyndon B. Johnson signed the Civil Rights Act into law. Among other things, this law made it illegal to deny a person a job based on their race, color, religion, sex, or national origin. It also prohibited discrimination when it came to promoting someone at work or firing them from their job.

Although these acts made discrimination in the workplace illegal, unfair practices still persist. For example, in the United States, white women who work at full-time jobs earn an average of 17 percent less than white men. Women of color make even less than white women. See for yourself in the chart on the right!

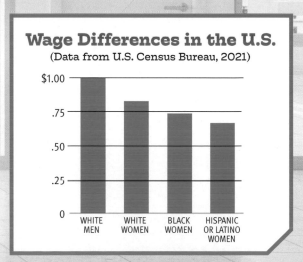

Wage Differences in the U.S.
(Data from U.S. Census Bureau, 2021)

In 2022, almost 30 percent of American kids ages 8 to 14 kept their money in a piggy bank.

Many families save for their children's college education.

Saving Money

The money we earn can be spent or saved. We spend our money on everyday needs and on things we want. When we save money, we put away some portion to use later. People often save money "for a rainy day." That means if an emergency happens—like a family's car breaks down—they have money to pay to fix the problem. People also save money for expensive purchases. For example, you might want a game that costs three times what you get as your allowance each month. If you save your money, eventually you will be able to buy the game.

Many Ways to Save

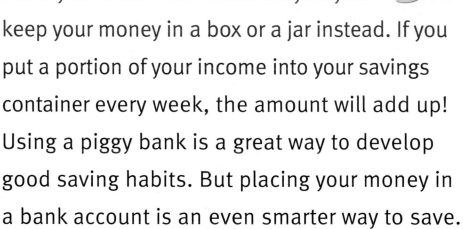

Do you have a piggy bank where you store your bills and coins? Maybe you keep your money in a box or a jar instead. If you put a portion of your income into your savings container every week, the amount will add up! Using a piggy bank is a great way to develop good saving habits. But placing your money in a bank account is an even smarter way to save.

Kids under 18 need to open an account with a parent or guardian.

Protecting Savings

In 1929, the world experienced an extreme financial crisis known as the Great Depression. Millions of Americans lost all their money when banks across the country failed. People had placed their savings in bank accounts. But when they tried to take their money out, it was gone. To keep that from ever happening again, President Franklin D. Roosevelt created the Federal Deposit Insurance Corporation (FDIC) in 1933. The FDIC provides insurance for people who use banks. Today, anyone who has money in a bank that is FDIC insured is guaranteed to get their money back from the government if the bank fails.

President Roosevelt (seated) signs banking legislation.

The FDIC insures your money up to $250,000.

Opening a Bank Account

A lot of banks have accounts that are intended especially for young people. To get started, you would **deposit** your money into the account. Then the bank would give you a **debit card**. You can use that card to make purchases at a store or online. You can also use the debit card at an automated teller machine (ATM) to take cash out of your account.

You need to make an initial deposit to open an account.

In 2022, almost 50 percent of teens in the United States had a bank account.

Grow Your Money

A savings account is one type of bank account that lets you earn **interest**. Interest is the payment you receive from the bank for the use of your money. Interest is paid over a certain period at a fixed percentage of the deposit amount. Let's pretend you have $100 in a savings account that earns 3.90 percent annual interest. At the end of one year, the amount in your account will have grown to $103.90.

"DO YOU REALIZE YOU'RE NOT EARNING ANY INTEREST ON THAT?"

Do you think a squirrel storing all of its acorns in a tree is similar to a person saving all their money in a piggy bank? Why or why not?

Accountants are professionals who help people with their taxes.

In 2022, the U.S. government collected 4.9 trillion dollars in tax revenue.

Paying Taxes

How much money we have left over from our earnings to spend or save is affected by taxes and tax rates. Taxes are payments the government can collect from people or businesses. In fact, taxes are the number one source of **revenue** for the government. Sales tax, income tax, and property tax are three common types of tax in the United States. Some of those taxes are paid to local and state governments. Others are paid to the federal government.

Many items we buy are taxed.

Sales Tax

Has this ever happened to you? You buy something at a store, and when the clerk rings up your item, the total cost doesn't match the number on the price tag. It's a little bit higher. That's because the store is charging you sales tax. Sales tax is usually a percentage of the sales price. For example, if you buy a shirt for $10 and the sales tax in your state is 3 percent, the total cost for the shirt will be $10.30 ($10 x .03 = 30¢ tax). The sales tax percentage, or rate, depends on where you live.

In the United States, four states do not charge sales tax: Delaware, Montana, New Hampshire, and Oregon.

Is Candy Essential?

Most state and local governments have something called a grocery exemption to the sales tax. That means that people do not have to pay sales tax on essential foods, like eggs, milk, flour, fruits, and vegetables. However, in many states, goods like soda and candy are taxed. Soda and candy are commonly excluded from the grocery exemption because they have little nutritional value and are therefore not essential grocery products. Do you think this is fair?

Income Tax

Income tax is a tax paid on the money a person earns. It is a percentage of their income. Most countries have a progressive tax system. The rate rises as taxable income rises. Using the examples from page 10, a doctor would pay a higher tax rate than a fast-food worker. A flat tax rate, which is less common, is a system where the same rate is used for everyone, regardless of income. In the same way, businesses also pay income taxes on their earnings.

"You get $5 for an allowance, is that after taxes?"

Employers take money from workers' paychecks to pay income tax to the government. The workers' take-home pay is the amount they make after taxes. Do you think allowances should also be taxed? Why or why not?

In the United States, three out of four people get a tax refund every year.

Income tax first started in the United States in 1862. The money was needed to help fight the Civil War.

Tax Day

Once a year all workers in the United States must submit an income tax return to the Internal Revenue Service (IRS). That government agency is responsible for collecting taxes. Those forms are usually due on or around April 15. Among other things, an income tax return shows a person's income for the year. Sometimes the IRS might tell the person that they have to pay more taxes. Sometimes people get some money back instead. That is called a tax refund.

In some states, both this home and the car would be taxed.

Property Tax

Property tax is also sometimes known as real estate tax. It is primarily a tax on a home or a piece of land that a person owns. The amount of tax is based on the value of the property. People in some states also pay property tax on luxury items such as boats and cars. As with income tax, both individuals and businesses pay property taxes.

How Are Taxes Used?

Taxes are an important source of revenue for federal, state, and local governments. (Local government refers to your town, village, or city.) The money is often spent on important services that benefit the people who pay the taxes. That can include paying to maintain roads and bridges; providing funds for public schools, parks, and health care; and paying for our military.

Tax revenue allows governments to hire workers like those shown here.

31

It is easy to see inflation in purchases we make every week, like groceries.

In September 2022, the cost of groceries was 13 percent higher than it had been the previous year.

Understanding Inflation

Inflation is an increase in the prices of many goods and services over time. Like taxes, inflation affects how much we can spend and save. As goods and services become more expensive, we can afford to buy fewer of them with the same amount of money. Salaries in the United States have increased over the past 40 years. But American workers' **purchasing power** has barely changed. That means that even though workers are making more money, they are not able to buy more goods.

Reasons for Inflation

Inflation can occur for a number of reasons. Prices can go up when the costs of raw materials rise. For example, a company that manufactures bicycles has to buy rubber, among other things, to make the bike tires. If the manufacturer has to spend more money to get the rubber, the company will have to charge more for the bike. Prices also go up when a business increases workers' wages or if many people want to buy something that has limited availability.

Many things go into the price of a bicycle.

High transportation costs, such as high gas prices, can also cause the prices of goods to rise.

Stores often discount items that are not selling well.

LEGO

CLEARANCE SALE

Great Discounts Up to

40%*

ALL MUST GO!

Promotion Period:
Starting 4 August 2017, while stocks last

Supply and Demand

Supply and demand plays a large role in determining the prices of things we buy, and it can also contribute to inflation. Supply is the amount of a product that is available. Demand is how many people want that product. If there is a lot of a product available but not many people want it, the price will likely go down. If there is a limited supply of a product and a lot of people want it, the price will likely go up.

How Does Inflation Affect Us?

As prices increase, purchasing power decreases. For example, let's pretend a family has budgeted $100 per week for groceries. That includes enough food for every breakfast, lunch, and dinner the family will eat during the week. If the cost of groceries increases by 10 percent before the family's next shopping trip, it will now cost $110 to buy the same groceries. Without the extra ten dollars to spend, the family will have to cut back on food purchases.

Timeline of Hyperinflation

1790s
FRANCE
Hyperinflation is an inflation rate of 50% or more per month. The first record of that happening is from the French Revolution, when monthly inflation reached a peak of 143%.

OCTOBER 1923
GERMANY
One reason for Germany's hyperinflation, which reached a high of 29,500% that month, was excessive printing of currency.

OCTOBER 1944
GREECE
World War II was one cause of Greece's hyperinflation, which peaked at 13,800% that month.

With inflation, many people are forced to spend more and save less. Also, if people think prices will continue to rise, they may try to buy more goods before that happens. Taking money away from savings means people might not have a cushion if an emergency arises.

The per-pound cost of chocolate chip cookies went from $1.49 in 1980 to $4.22 in 2022.

FIRST HALF OF 1946
HUNGARY
Huge debt contributed to a peak inflation of 13,600,000,000,000,000,000% during those six months.

JANUARY 1994
YUGOSLAVIA
Wars and destabilization led to a peak inflation of 313,000,000%.

NOVEMBER 2008
ZIMBABWE
Mismanagement by the government led to a 79,600,000,000% peak inflation.

Source: Paul Toscano, "The Worst Hyperinflation Situations of All Time." CNBC.com

How Is Inflation Measured?

One way experts measure inflation is by using the Consumer Price Index (CPI). Every month, the U.S. government gathers the prices of 80,000 consumer items, which include everything from housing and groceries to health care. The CPI measures the change in the price of those items. It is used by both individuals and businesses as a guide in making economic decisions. For example, in September 2022, the annual rate of inflation was 8.2 percent year over year. That means that prices rose an average of 8.2 percent from a year earlier.

The father in this cartoon is talking about inflation and purchasing power. Can you think of something you buy regularly—like a snack or a drink—that has gone up in price since last year? How much has the price changed?

Smart Choices

People work so that they have money to pay for necessities like food, housing, and clothes. They also work so they have money to spend on "extras"—like movies, restaurants, and vacations—as well as money to save. Just as important as making money is understanding how the money we make and the money we can save are affected by outside forces like taxes and inflation. The more you know about how finances work in the real world, the more successful you will be.

It's never too soon to start practicing smart saving strategies.

Understanding Patterns

Experts work with data and often try to find patterns in graphs in order to better understand the economy. Imagine you work at an ice cream company and are interested in studying the trends in prices of ice cream over the years. Study the graph and answer the questions.

Average Ice Cream Prices in the U.S.

PRICE PER HALF GALLON

$6.00 — $5.70
$5.00 — $4.89
$4.00 — $3.90
$3.00
$2.00 — $2.10 $2.58
$1.00
0

DATE: 1982   1992   2002   2012   2022

Analyze It!

1 In which year was the price of ice cream highest?

2 At which point did the biggest increase in price occur?

    a. From 1982 to 1992
    b. From 1992 to 2002
    c. From 2002 to 2012
    d. From 2012 to 2022

3 What is the difference in the price of ice cream from September 1982 to September 2022?

4 Based on the trend shown here, what do you think the price of ice cream will be in 2032?

    a. Less than $5.70
    b. $5.70
    c. More than $5.70

ANSWERS: 1. 2022; **2.** b; **3.** $3.60; **4.** c

41

Making a Budget for Your Business

A budget is an essential part of a business plan. To learn how to make one, pretend you are going to set up a lemonade stand for a day. Once you learn the steps for your lemonade stand budget, you can apply them to any business you can think of!

Materials

Paper

Marker or pen

Your favorite lemonade recipe

Internet (to check prices)

Calculator

Directions

1 On a piece of paper, use a marker or pen to draw a T-chart like the one shown on page 43. This will be your budget.

2 Look for a lemonade recipe and see how many cups it yields, or makes. Then decide how many cups you might realistically sell in one day. You can increase or decrease the recipe as necessary to get to the total cups of lemonade you have available for sale.

3 Begin by writing everything you will need for your business on the left side of the chart. Start with the ingredients to make the lemonade. Will you need to buy a pitcher and cups to serve the lemonade? List those items too. They are your supplies.

BUDGET

ITEM	COST
INGREDIENTS	
☐ Lemons	$ _____
☐ Sugar	$ _____
SUPPLIES	
☐ Pitcher	$ _____
☐ Paper cups	$ _____
WORKERS	
☐ One helper	$ _____
MARKETING	
☐ Poster board	$ _____
☐ Construction paper	$ _____
TOTAL COST	$ _____
Cost per cup	$ _____

4 Will you need help running your lemonade stand? If so, add workers to the left side of the chart. How will you advertise your lemonade stand? Will you make a sign? Hand out flyers? These are marketing costs. Add them to the left side of your chart.

5 On the right side of your T-chart, write down the cost of each item on your list. Add everything together to see how much money you will have to spend to start your business. This is your total cost. To find out your cost per cup, divide your total cost by the number of cups of lemonade you are making.

6 Now decide how much you want to charge per cup. For example, you can charge 10 cents or 25 cents over cost. How many cups would you have to sell to cover your costs? What would your total profit be if you sold all the lemonade?

Percentage of children in the United States who get an allowance: About 61 percent

Percentage of budget the average U.S. household spends on housing: 33.8 percent

Percentage of U.S. households that have at least one bank account: 95.5 percent

Average amount of refund U.S. workers get back from their tax return each year: $3,000

Note: These statistics are as of 2022.

Did you find the truth?

F The price of chocolate chip cookies has not changed in the past 40 years.

T People with jobs pay income tax.

Resources

Other books in this series:

  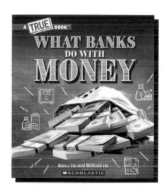

You can also look at:

Adler, David A. *Money Madness*. New York: Holiday House, 2009.

Furgang, Kathy. *Everything Money*. Washington, D.C.: National Geographic Kids, 2013.

Sember, Brette McWhorter. *The Everything Kids' Money Book: Earn It, Save It, and Watch It Grow!* Avon, MA: Adams Media, 2008.

Thornton, J. D. *How to Make Money*. New York: Scholastic, 2006.

Glossary

currency (KUR-uhn-see) the form of money used in a country

debit card (DEB-it KAHRD) a plastic card that is connected to a bank account and that can be used to pay for things

deposit (di-PAH-zit) to put money into a bank account

entrepreneur (ahn-truh-pruh-NUR) someone who starts businesses and finds new ways to make money

goods (GUDZ) things that are sold or things that someone owns

income (IN-kuhm) the money that a person earns or receives, especially from working

interest (IN-trist) a fee paid for borrowing money, usually a percentage of the amount borrowed, as well as money paid to you by a bank for keeping your savings there

profit (PRAH-fit) the amount of money left after all the costs of running a business have been subtracted from the money earned

purchasing power (PUR-chuh-sing POU-ur) the value of money based on how much it can buy

revenue (REV-uh-noo) the money that a government gets from taxes and other sources

salary (SAL-ur-ee) the fixed amount of money someone is paid for their work

services (SUR-vih-sez) a system or way of providing something useful

Index

Page numbers in **bold** indicate illustrations.

About the Authors

Janet Liu (top) and Melinda Liu (bottom) are sisters who are passionate about economic and financial literacy for young people. They are the founders of the nonprofit organization J&M Sunrizon Economics and the creators of the Wonderland Economics YouTube channel. Janet and Melinda are also the authors of *Elementary Economics* and *Economics for Tweens*, and are currently undergrads studying economics, computer science, and management at the Massachusetts Institute of Technology (MIT).